Swing Trading Strategies

3 Simple and Profitable Strategies for Beginners

Table of Contents

Introduction

Congratulations on purchasing this book and thank you for doing so.

The following chapters will discuss everything that you need to know to get started with swing trading. Swing trading is the perfect combination of day trading and long-term investing. You will be able to make money over a few weeks, but you will not need to spend all your time online trying to learn the market and hoping that the market goes your way like with day trading. If you are interested in learning how to work with swing trading and how to see results, then this guidebook has all the information that you need to get started.

Inside this guidebook, you will learn what swing trading is all about, the benefits of swing trading, and even how to get started in the market. You will then learn the three best strategies that you can try out if you want to see real profits with swing trading. Whether you are a beginner to investing or you have been in the market for some time and want to try out something new, this guidebook will help you to see success.

When you are ready to get started with swing trading and making money in no time with the stock market, make sure to check out this guidebook to help you get started.

There are plenty of books on this subject on the market, thanks again for choosing this one! Every effort was made to ensure it is full of as much useful information as possible, please enjoy!

Chapter 1:

What is Swing Trading?

Investing can be a smart way to watch your money grow. You can put your money to work and earn some more in the process without having to go back to working another job. Depending on the type of investment you choose to go with, you could end up making a lot of money in the process without doing a ton of work. Learning how to pick out a good investment opportunity that will make you as much money as possible while also limiting your risks can be a challenge. Luckily, there are a lot of options that you can work with and the risk can be limited as long as you learn the proper methods to be successful in them.

For those investors who are looking to get into the market and want to earn some money in a short amount of time, working with swing trading may be the right option. Swing trading works because it tries to capture all the gains possible with a stock, or any financial instrument that you choose, within a hold that lasts either overnight or a few weeks. This type of investment is going to be short-term, which means that you will not hold onto this investment for many years like you would your retirement plan. However, many investors prefer this option over day trading because they get some more time to work the market and can limit their risks.

Those who are working with swing trading will often work with the fundamental or intrinsic value of the stock. They will also need to take some time to look at the price trends and other patterns that come with a stock because this helps them to make some good decisions for which stocks will make a profit with swing trading.

So, you may be curious how a swing trader is going to work compared to investors in other opportunities. To begin with, all swing traders are going to act quickly because they need to be able to find situations where a stock is about to move upwards over a short amount of time. It does not matter how that stock will do over time. If there is a big piece of news that is about to happen with a stock that will drive the price up for at least a few days, then these are the ones that you want to work within swing trading.

To see the biggest profits, these upward trends need to be something that is out of the ordinary. Otherwise, lots of other investors are going to jump into the market as well and your profits will be limited. You will need to look at the history of the stock, some of the news that is surrounding the stock, and other factors to determine that this particular stock is going to have a big upward trend for you to capitalize on. If you are right, you will purchase the stock at a low price and then sell it within the next few weeks in order to make a nice profit.

There are some similarities between a swing trader and a day trading, especially considering that the individuals who do both will work this kind of market on their own from home. You are not going to have a big financial institution that is working with this option because the movement is too quick and the profits from each trade may not be huge. The point here is that when you do quite a few of these trades over a few weeks, your profit will add up. But the individual trades may be small on their own.

As a day trader, you are going to hold onto either a position that is long or one that is short. You will not hold this position for a long time. Most traders will get rid of the stock within a few days, but you can hold onto the stock for up to a few weeks and still be considered a swing trader.

You are assuming that there is going to be a large price move in the stock, so you need to be careful about picking out the position you want to work with or your risk will not be limited. In addition, if you are working with some time frame charts, you need to rely on some that take on longer ranges, like daily and weekly charts, to help you determine how the market is going to behave.

Day trading vs. swing trading

If you have done any research into trading, you have most likely heard about day trading and may be wondering how day trading and swing trading are different from each other. Both of these strategies are going to watch for trends in the stock market and will try to capitalize on this information to make a profit in the short-term.

There are some big differences that you will find between day trading and swing trading. One difference is the amount of time that you are going to hold onto the position you chose. When you work with day trading, you are going to purchase a stock and then sell that same stock all in one day before the market closes. You may do it early in the morning and then sell at the end, or only hold onto the position for a few hours, but your purchases and sales will happen all at the same time. On the other hand, when you work in swing trading you are going to hold onto your position overnight at a minimum. You are able to hold onto that position for up to two weeks and still it would be considered swing trading.

In some cases, this can add in some more risk to the trades that you are completing. It is really hard to know what is going to happen in the stock market when you leave your position alone overnight. This is why a lot of swing traders are going to work with smaller position sizes compared to what the day traders would do.

With swing trading, you will get a bit of choice on how long you will hold the position, which is a good way to reduce your risk a bit. However, it is always in your best interests to set up a timeline for how long you want to be in the market before you start your investment. Looking over the charts to get some information and forming a good idea of how the market will behave in the next few weeks will make it easier to come up with a plan for when to enter the market and when to get out to make your profit. Being able to do this will make it easier to keep your emotions out of the investment and can minimize your risk since you know exactly what is going to happen.

As a swing trader, you will have a number of responsibilities. You first will need to look at the chart patterns of your trade over many days. There are some different patterns that you will need to look for including triangles, head and shoulders patterns, moving average crossovers, flags, and even cup and handle patterns. Looking at these patterns, as well as developing a good strategy, can make a big difference in the results that you will see because you will learn how to recognize ups and downs in the market.

Swing trading is going to have more risk than some of the longer -term options that you may choose to go with. With the long-term investments, you will find that you have the time and the relaxation to not worry about the big ups and downs in the market as much. Your account will end up evening out if you stay on the market long enough.

But with swing trading, this is not always going to work. You are only going to be in the market for up to a few weeks at the most. This means that if a trend does not go your way, you are going to lose out on money. You must do your research diligently before starting and make sure that you are able to accurately read the market. You only get a few weeks, which is more than what a day trader will get to work with, but this adds in more risk, especially when you are working in an overnight position.

When it comes time to invest your money, you will have a lot of choices that you can make. You can choose to work on your own retirement plan or you can go with a short-term option that will make you money right now. But when it comes to swinging trading, you get the best of both worlds. You can minimize your risk while still being able to make a lot of money over a few weeks.

How a swing trader thinks

Before you decide to use swing trader as your method of investing, you need to make sure that you have the right kind of mindset. If you go into the investment with the wrong thought process, it is going to be very difficult to make any money in the process. You may go into this investment hoping to make a good amount of money, but if you see this is a long-term investment, like your retirement plan, or you don't have the time to watch the market and stick it out, then this is not going to be the best option for you.

When you are working with swing trading, you have to remember that all of the steps of the investment will occur within a few weeks. You may decide to stick with swing trading for many years and turn this into an income, but the individual trades never last more than a few weeks at most. If you are doing swing trading and the trades take longer than the few weeks, you have exited out of swing trading and the strategy is not going to work as well for you. There are some big differences between long-term and short-term investing and it will take a specific type of trader to see success when they are working with a swing trader.

So, what does a swing trader need to have, what kind of personality, in order to be successful? First, they need to be able to think things through without emotions. Things can change quickly when you are a day trader and your money can often be at risk. Since you are not working with the investment for the long-term, it is possible to lose that money quickly without a chance to gain it back. This can be hard on a lot of new investors and can often negatively influence the trades that they make.

There are some people who have a lot of trouble keeping their emotions out of their trades. These people are going to get too caught up in the moment and will make some bad trading decisions. This leads them to lose out on a lot of money, money that they could have held onto if they had gone through and thought out their trades the right way. If you are not able to control your emotions during these trades, then it is best to find another investment option other than swing trading.

Another thing that you will need to be aware of is that you need to love looking through charts and doing research. You will never make any money with swing trading if you don't perform some good research ahead of time. You will miss out on important trends, get into a stock at the wrong time, and worst of all, lose money. Often these things would be easy to see happening if you had just done your research ahead of time. It is important to look at the charts for any stock that you are interested in, as well as look at the charts for the overall market as well. This helps you to see what is going to happen in the future and will make it easier to form predictions before starting your investment.

As a swing trader, you need to have a good sense for making predictions. It doesn't do you any good to enter a trade when the upswing is already occurring. This is often too late to enter the trade and you will pay too much for the stock and may not be able to sell it for a profit. To make the most money, you have to find a stock that is currently undervalued, one that isn't being bought that much right now, so that you can purchase it for a lower price than what it is worth.

You do not want to go for a stock just because it is low, though. You need to pick out a stock that is undervalued. This means that it may be selling for less than it is worth right now, but there is something that will happen in the near future that will raise the price of the stock back to its market value or higher. When this uptrend occurs again, you will be able to sell the stock and make a profit. With the right prediction, you will be able to do this within a few weeks and earn a good amount of profit in a short amount of time. If you enter into swing trading and you have trouble reading charts and recognizing when a new trend is about to happen, you are going to miss out on a lot of potential profits because you won't trade the right stocks.

Should I get into swing trading?

There are many different options that come with investing and picking the one that works the best for you can sometimes be a challenge. You want to make sure that you are picking out an investment strategy that will actually help you to make money and will match up with your own personal goals. There are too many people who decide to go into swing trading because they think it is an easy way to make money without wasting a lot of time. This can be true, but there is also some work that you have to put in to see this profit.

Many of those who go into swing trading do it after trying out day trading. They were interested in the fast-paced world of day trading and maybe they saw all the profits that others were making and saw this as appealing. However, once they got into the market, they found that it took up too much of their time. They had to spend all day worrying about the little ups and downs in the market and often they wouldn't have any free time in order to get anything else done.

Working in day trading can be really stressful for most people. Even those who may be able to handle the stress found that this is not an investment type that they enjoyed all that much because of all the risk. They went over to swing trading because they are still able to use a lot of the same strategies from day trading and they are still able to make a good profit margin. But there is the benefit of getting more time with the trades and not having to waste your whole life in front of a computer in the hopes of making a profit.

If you are going into swing trading because you think it will make you rich quickly, then choose another investment option. Yes, there are people who are able to do swing trading and make a ton of money in just a few weeks, but this is outside the norm. It is going to take some consistency and a lot of hard work in order to make a good income from swing trading and many beginners are going to lose money when they first start. Those who go in and make rash decisions and don't think things through will end up losing all of their money in the process.

On the other hand, those who get into day trading in order to invest their money, those who are interested in learning the skills of the trade and understand there are some risks to swing trading, are the ones who will see success. If you don't have the mindset of this being an investment and you are not ready to make quick and informed decisions for your trades, then swing trading can end up being a money pit for you.

Swing trading is a bit different than some of the other trading options that you may choose to go with. It is fast-paced, can bring in a lot of emotions along the way, and has the potential for a lot of profits if you learn how to do it the right way. But when you learn the different strategies and have a lot of the mindset requirements above, you can see a lot of success when it comes to swing trading.

Chapter 2:

The Benefits of Swing Trading

As we mentioned before, there are a lot of investments that you can choose to go with. Some people like to stick with long-term investments because it can help to set them up for a good retirement and takes out a lot of the risk that they are dealing with. Some people like to work in real estate and do rental properties and flipping houses. You may even just like to start your own business, work in the stock market, or work with digital currencies. With all of these options available, you may be curious as to why you would want to work with swing trading and not one of the other options.

Many people like to work with swing trading because it allows them the option to earn money quickly. Sure, there are more risks, but you could bring home a profit in a few weeks rather than having to wait years before you can touch your money. Plus, you don't have to worry about dealing with tenants or trying to make the bills each month when you work with swing trading like you would with real estate. There are a lot of benefits that you will be able to enjoy when you choose swing trading for your investment option, including:

- Lower risk compared to day trading: When you compare the amount of risk that you are taking with swing trading compared to day trading, it is much lower with the former. This is because you are going to have some more time to work on the market. Sometimes it is hard to estimate how the market is going to do in one day because there is a lot of up and down movement based on how other traders are behaving that day. But it is easier for a lot of traders to predict whether their stock is going to do better over a couple of days, especially if there is some big news coming out about the company. This lower risk is going to make swing trading a more profitable option for many traders.

- Do swing trading and other trades: Many traders like swing trading because they can do these trades along with day trading. During market hours for the day, the trader may focus a lot of their energy on the position they took for day trading and then focus on the swing trade later on. They can do this by placing their swing trade position the night before, or at least before the market opens that day. This helps to prevent confusion while trading.

- Having the advantage of trading overnight: Some traders find that trading overnight is a risky endeavor and that it is going to harm their profits. They worry that there is going to be a big trend that occurs overnight and that they will be able to do nothing about it because they are asleep. Sometimes there are a few gaps that will occur overnight and whether they will go with your trade or not will vary. In many cases, this overnight position is going to help you out, giving you more time to wait for the trend and make big profits the next day.

- Time to look at the market: With day trading, you are only able to look at the market over one single day. If something starts to go wrong with your trade, you don't have a lot of time to wait for it to turn around. Even if the market is going to go the way you predict, that may not happen until the next day and you would miss out on day trading. With swing trading, you can stay in the market a little bit longer and wait for that uptrend to happen, even if it happens to take a few extra days to get there. This helps to reduce the risk and can make many investors more comfortable with using this option.

- Potential to reach the trades better. When you compare this to day trading, you are more likely to reach the trade that you want when using swing trading. You get more time to watch how the market will behave, to predict the trades and how they will behave over a longer period of time, and you can end up making more money in the process. In fact, you can even make a lot of money overnight if you choose the right stocks at the right time with this trading method. Or if your position needs to be held over a few days rather than a few hours, swing trading can make this happen.

- Freedom throughout the day: For those who have tried out day trading in the past, you know how much of a time commitment it can all be. You literally need to spend your whole day watching the trade. And when little changes happen, whether they are up or down changes, they can make big differences in how well you will do in day trading. This can be stressful and can turn a lot of people away from even giving it a try. Those who go with swing trading often are ones who tried out day trading and didn't like all the work and stress that went with it. They wanted to still make some good money over the short-term, without needing to spend all their day in front of a computer screen watching how the market was doing.

There are a lot of reasons why day trading and swing trading are similar and why they attract the same kind of person to investing in them. With that said, there are also many reasons why swing trading is more beneficial to the investor making money than working with day trading. With more options, more freedom, and a better chance at seeing success, swing trading may be the stock option investment that will work the best for you.

Chapter 3:

How to Begin with Swing Trading

Now that we have taken some time to learn about swing trading, you may be interested in getting into the market and using this strategy to make some money. While hearing a bit about swing trading is good and can help you to get interested in this option, you need to do a bit more than that. You have to have an idea of which strategy to go with, how to find a good broker who can help you to get into the market and will give you some advice, and learn how to get into the market and exit at the right time.

So, one of the first things that you need to concentrate on is finding a broker to work with. The broker is going to make a big difference in how well a beginner is able to do with their trades, so you need to pick someone you trust and who will do the work that you want. This broker will be able to place your trades for you, will offer up advice when it is needed and can be there whenever you have questions or concerns. There are several broker types that you can pick from and often the choice that you make will depend on which features you would like them to offer. You can also pick your broker based on how much help you need from the broker and how much you want to spend on them.

The next goal for you as a swing trader is to figure out what tools you want to use to help analyze the market. It is best if you are able to put a few of these tools in place because it will help you to make better predictions. If you find that there are the same indicators in the market on two or more of these tools, it is more likely that you can make the prediction and make money. The strategy that you pick will also help you to determine which tools you are going to use.

After you have gone and picked out the right tools to use for watching the market, you also need to spend a bit of time researching the market and learning how the market, as well as your tools, will work. This is another place where your broker can come in handy. They will be able to talk about the market with you are looking to invest in and can even show you how to get started with using some of the analytical tools. The more research and experimenting that you are able to do ahead of time, the more likely you will be able to make a profit when you get started with swing trading.

The next step that you can work on is to choose which strategy fits your trading needs. There are a lot of great strategies available to pick from and all of them have the potential to make you money as long as you use them the proper way. If you don't really learn your method of trading properly or you switch up strategies in the middle of a trade, you are going to end up with a mess on your hands. Picking out one strategy, sticking with it, and really learning how to make it work is the best way that you can make money with swing trading over the long-term.

Choosing a good strategy is probably going to be one of the hardest things to do. They all work differently and will require you to look at the charts in a different way than the others. And if you mess up with a strategy or you try to mix it up in the middle of a trade, you will end up losing a lot of money in the process. This can be stressful for someone who is new to the swing trading business. Make sure you fully learn how each strategy is supposed to work and even discuss some of them with your broker ahead of time to help you pick the right one.

You also need to take the time to get started with your trades. Your broker will be able to help you out with this part. They can either give you advice on the trades that you are going to work with or you can tell them the rules that you want to follow. Either way, it is best for them to put the trades in for you since they can get the work done quickly.

When you are ready to place your trades, it is important that you work with what is known as stop points. You need to have two stop points in place; one for losing money and one for earning money. These points are so important because they are the points where you are going to exit the market when they are hit and they are helpful in reducing your risk. For example, if the market goes down and reaches your low stop point, it means that you need to exit the market and take your losses.

This is hard for some beginners who see that they are losing money and would rather stay in and try to get the money back. But this often leads you to make rash decisions that will lose more money than before. Sticking with the stop points may seem silly, but it is really important in helping you to reduce your risks and actually see results.

You need a stopping point on the other side of things as well. This helps you to get your profits and know when you should leave the market, even if the market goes back up. Since you are trading over a short amount of time, you want to ensure that you will reach your profits without losing money if things reverse. Putting this stop point in place will help you to make as much profit as possible while reducing your risk as well.

When the trade has been successful, you can be done with your first round of swing trading. Some of the trades will happen overnight and others are going to take a few weeks to accomplish, but most of the time you will complete your trade and earn your profit in a relatively short time period. You can then take your profit and move on to your next trade.

Swing trading tips

As with any investment type, there are going to be some risks when it comes to swing trading. If you want to be able to make a lot of money over a short amount of time, this is the option that you need to go with. However, since it is so short-term, there is some risk that you will deal with when working in swing trading. Understanding the best time to get into the market and learning how to read the charts can certainly make the whole process easier and will make it so you earn a profit in no time. as a beginner, it can be challenging to know how to behave in the market and which steps to take to reduce your risk and see the best results. Some of the best tips that you can follow to do well with swing trading include:

- Pick a good strategy: As a beginner, you may think that you need to go with a complex strategy. Beginners might think that they need this kind of strategy because it will increase their chances of seeing profits. However, these complex strategies are difficult to learn to use. In many cases, going for a complicated strategy will make it difficult to make any profit because you won't understand what you are doing. It is much better to go with a simple strategy that you understand rather than a complicated strategy that makes you lose money.

- Start in one place: It may be tempting to work in several markets at once. You may assume that this will make you more money than just working in one. But as you are learning how to work with swing trading, it can make things too confusing when you work with more than one industry at a time. As a beginner, start with one industry, learn how to work it well, and then expand out when you feel ready.

- Add in a stop loss: This is a big reason that you are going to lose your money. If you don't put a stop loss in place, you can easily lose a lot of money because the market goes down. Whether the market goes down when you aren't watching it or because you are trying to regain your losses, you can end up losing more money than you can afford. Add in a stop loss at the place where you are comfortable with losing money, and then get out of the market once you reach that number.

- Trade both directions if possible: To ensure that you are going to make money with swing trading is to make sure that you trade both positions. Trading on one side or the other is going to make you miss out on at least half the opportunities to make money.

- Think about the risk to reward ratio: This ratio needs to be at least one to three. Remember that you are trading short term, so you will not make a ton of money in the process. You can make a decent profit, but you won't make many thousands over this time. Ensure that you stay with a good risk to reward ratio so that you will make some money without losing everything.

- Keep the emotions out of it: As soon as the emotions come into play with swing trading, you have started to lose. There are too many people who don't follow the advice of others and will choose to just jump into the market and hope it all works out. But then they will start to lose money and not know how to act. In many cases, you will start to make rash decisions in the hopes that you can regain the money that you lost, but this often goes the other way. Even if you are making a profit, you may stay in the market too long, and when it turns around, you lose out on money instead of earning money. Learn how to keep your emotions out of the game by having a good plan in place and sticking with it.

- Pick out a broker: As a beginner, having someone on your side who can answer your questions and help you make important decisions can make all the difference. Many people are surprised by all the hard work that comes with swing trading and they are not sure how to handle it all. With a broker, you have someone who wants you to succeed, so they will provide you with the information you need to make this happen.

- Take advice, but come up with your own plan: There are many ways to do swing trading and learning from others who are successful can help you to win.

However, you need to come up with your own strategy to get the best results. If you just blindly follow what others tell you to do, you will make big mistakes that will cost you a lot of money.

- Take a look at the indicators of the market: The market indicators are going to help you figure out which way you should trade and which stocks you should stick with. There are many tools that you can use to analyze the market and you can pick some of your own or ask your broker to see which ones they have available. Some of the indicators are better to use for long-term investments, you can still find out a lot of information when it comes to your swing trading strategy.

- You can't control the market: No matter how much you try, you do not have control over how the market behaves. Just because you traded a certain way doesn't mean that the market is going to listen to you. Just because you are losing money doesn't mean the market is going to change and do what you want. Since the market is not going to behave the way that you would like, it is your job to look through your analysis tools and then pick out trades that go with the market, rather than against the market.

As a beginner, you may be worried about picking out trades that are going to work. This is a different type of trading than you may be used to in the past, but it can really help you to make money if you learn how to read and trade in the market the right way. If you want to see success with this short-term investment and actually make money, make sure that you follow the tips above and you are sure to win.

Chapter 4:

Strategy One – Breakouts
and Breakdowns

As you get used to working with swing trading, you will find that not all of the patterns that you observe in a stock chart are going to be equal. As you look at the charts, you will notice that there are hundreds of stock chart patterns and some of them can be successful and some lead to nowhere. The channel breakout is a good option to go with because it is a basic strategy that many beginners like to move towards, even if they started out with a different strategy.

One of the reasons that a lot of beginners like to go with breakout strategies is because of the increased momentum and volatility that will come with them in most cases. Although it is going to help you increase how much profit you can potentially make, it can also help to increase your risk as well, so you need to be careful. In addition, some of the strategies are going to show false breakouts, which manes that your percentage of winning trades to losing trades will be low. But if you do this strategy the right way, you are going to earn a lot of money with swing trading.

Learning how to avoid these false breakouts is critical if you want to make money with this strategy rather than losing most of the time. The first thing that you should look out for is a market that is trending. The biggest reason for one of these false breakouts is that you are following signals that are against what the main trend of the market is doing. When you pay attention to the market and follow the trend that is going on, you will increase the percentage of times that you win.

So, for a breakout, you need to first find stocks, or another market, that has been seeing a strong trend for a few weeks or more. The trend can be either up or down as long as you see that it has been around for a few weeks or more. Once you see the stocks that have one of these trends, you need to take a look at the resistance levels and short-term support for a strong gap that is in the direction of the trend you are dealing with. The gaps that you want to work with are going to occur at the opening bell and there will be a strong amount of momentum and volatility present.

At this point, the setup is triggered and you are able to place the market order that will let you actually enter the trade. You want to make sure that before you enter the market, the gap that you are looking at is followed by strong volume and that the momentum that you are looking at is only pushing at the stock in one direction. The way that you tell this is by looking at the opening of the stock and then see how far against the opening price the stock ends up going.

After you have been able to enter your position, it is important to place a stop loss. The stop is going to help prevent you from losing out on more money than you can afford to lose at a time and lets you limit your risk a little bit more while trading. You should consider placing the stop halfway between your entry point and the closing price from the day before. Let's say that the difference between the opening price this morning and the previous closing price is $3.00, you would then want to add $1.50 to your entry price and this can be the stop loss or the buy stop to keep you safe.

You will start out the trade by looking for a stock that has been trending pretty strongly in one direction. It doesn't matter if the trend is going up or down, but you want to make sure that it is trending pretty strongly in the same direction. The better the trend is, the higher the odds that this breakout is going to happen in the same direction so always be careful about that. You do not want to pick out market tops and bottoms when you are a beginner and you always want to make sure you are going with the main trend when it comes to using this strategy.

After you have found a strong trend by looking through the charts and tables that you have, you need to take a look at the resistance levels and the daily support. If the trend you are working with is up to you then you only need to pay attention to the resistance levels. But if the trend is going down, then you must make sure that you pay attention to the support levels. These are both important levels with the breakout, so you need to know exactly where they are located to see success.

As a beginner, you may find that there are markets that move really quickly on you. You shouldn't be afraid of entering a position that moves quickly. You should be comfortable enough with the market that you are able to execute it right away and then know what you should do after the opening bell. That way, if the positions move quickly, you are all ready to take advantage and still make your money.

You will find as a trader that planning ahead, and keeping some detailed notes of what you are doing (especially about information for your resistance and support levels), can help you move fast, especially if the momentum is going strong in one direction. It is also a good idea to look at intra-day and daily charts so that you can always monitor the action of our trade, especially when you are already in the market. With all of this information in place, you are going to be set no matter how quickly the position moves.

Once that position is filled, the stop loss will then be placed as we talked about before; in between the closing price from the previous day and your current entry price. You will find that for the most part, the trade is not going to end up back at that level as long as the trend continues and you picked the right stock. This is going to provide you with some protection in case the worst situation occurs, but it most likely won't get to that point if you are dealing with a true breakout. Remember that you need to maintain this position at least overnight in order to gain the most opportunity for movement and profits in the right direction.

From the beginning, you should have an idea of how long you will stay in the market. The breakout is often going to be over a fairly short period of time. You will not stay in the market that long because the breakout is likely to reverse and will go back to its normal place in no time. But looking for that upward trend will help you to determine if a breakout is about to happen. And looking at the charts and the history of your stock will help you to get a good idea of what length of time you need to stay in the market before getting your breakout and the profits.

Remember that you need to go with the main trend of the stock if you would like to see a true breakout. If the stock has been going steadily downwards, it does not make sense to bet on a breakout happening that goes upward. This is not going to happen and is going against the main trend of the stock. Doing this is going to lead to disastrous results and you will lose money. It is always best to go with the main trend of the market in order to determine which stocks are going to see the breakouts.

Of course, you can choose to go with either trend that you would like. You may see this as a strategy that works the best if the market is going up, but there are breakouts that can occur when the market goes down as well. A market may start to see some downward trends and a lot of people are going to become worried about that stock and will try to get out of it before they lose too much money. If you place the right bet on this type of trend, you can easily make some money in the process as well.

Working with breakouts can be tricky. You need to be able to look through the market and see that a breakout is about to happen. If you wait until it is already occurring, you will end up missing out, paying too much money for the stocks, and perhaps not being able to get out of the market fast enough to make a profit. But there are times when the information you see on the charts can lead to a false breakout. This is an effective strategy as long as you follow the steps that are in this chapter for picking out a good stock and you take your time learning how to read the market indicators for a good investment.

Chapter 5:

Strategy Two – Options Strategy

Another beginner's strategy that you may want to go with is the options strategy. This approach is really easy to work with and it can limit your risk while increasing your profits in swing trading. There are three benefits of doing the options strategy. First, you will be able to make a lot of profit even from your first trade, which can be a blessing for those who are just getting started. If you pick a good option, you will be able to limit the risk that you are dealing with on the trade. And the third benefit is that you are able to trade on some higher price stocks even if your own account is pretty small.

As a beginner, you may not have a ton of money to initially invest in this strategy. You want to build up a bit and then put profits towards the investment later on, but your initial investment is not going to be as high as you would like. The options strategy is going to be a good one to use for this because you can leverage the initial amount that you have to invest. Basically, this means that you will not need to have a ton of capital present in order to trade on this strategy.

When you get started with the options strategy, you will stick with basic calls and puts options to make it easier. To keep it simple, if you would like to buy a particular stock, you are going to buy a call option. Then if you would like to sell a stock, you would purchase a put option.

Working with options can be a great way to get into the market as a beginner. You do not need to put the full amount of the value of the assets down to begin, which means that you need less capital. However, you are able to sell at the higher price later on and keep the profit, which can be nice for growing your portfolio and making a lot of money.

Options are going to be a derivative of security because the price of these options will be linked to the price of something else. Options can be considered a contract that will grant the investor the right to sell or purchase an underlying asset at a set price on or before an agreed upon date. The investor is not obligated to purchase or sell that asset if they do not want to though, so this helps to save you money if something doesn't go as you had planned. The right for the investor to buy is known as the call option and the right for them to sell is known as the put option.

When we are talking about a call option, you can think about it as a deposit for a future purpose. Let's say that you were a land developer who wanted to purchase a vacant lot at some point in the future, but only if some zoning laws that are being discussed are actually put into place. One thing that you can do is purchase a call option from the landowner to purchase the lot for a certain price at any point in the next three years.

Of course, the landowner wants to be able to get something out of this as well, so as the developer, you will need to put in a down payment to lock in the right that keeps the land at one price. For this one, we'll say that you want to purchase the land for $250,000 at some point during the next three years and you will pay a premium of $6,000 to the landowners.

Now a few years have passed and the zoning laws that you were waiting for are approved. You can then exercise the option and purchase the land for that agreed upon $250,000.

This price will remain the same, even if the market value of the plot doubles. On the other hand, the zoning approval may not come through until after the three years. If this happens, the expiration date has passed on the options and the developer will have to give up the $6,000 they put down as a premium and they must pay the market price (or more if there are many people interested in the land) if they wish to purchase the land.

You can also work with a put option. This one is more of an insurance policy on the investment that you work with. For this one, the land developer owns a big portfolio of stocks and is worried that signs are pointing towards a recession over the next few years. The developer wants to make sure that their portfolio is not going to lose over 10 percent of its value over this time.

Let's say that the S&P 500 is trading at 2500 currently, the developer is able to purchase this put option, which would allow them the right to sell the index at 2250 whenever they would like over the next two years. So, if the market crashes by 20 percent in six months, which is 500 points of the developer's portfolio, they have still made 250 points by being able to sell the index at the higher price. With the right put option, the developer could technically see the market drop down to zero and they will only lose ten percent of their portfolio. There is a premium with this option and you will lose that premium if the market doesn't drop, but it is a good way to protect your overall investment.

These are just examples of how you are able to work with the call and the put options. The first thing that you will notice is that when you purchase one of these options, you have the right, but not the obligation, to do something with it by a certain time. it is always possible for the investor to let their expiration date go by and let the option become worthless if they would like. But remember, when you let this happen, you are losing all of your investment, or the amount that you use to pay the premium of the option.

Also, remember that when you are working with options, these options are merely contracts that will have an underlying asset with them. This is why options are considered derivatives. Once you decide to execute your right to use the option, the contract will be executed for you. But you always have the option to back out if things do not go the way that you would like, just be aware that you will lose your initial investment if you do this so there is still some risk involved.

The main reason that many people like these are because they provide them with the opportunity to purchase an item at a lower price and then they can sell it for more later on. If you see a stock that is about to go up a lot in price in the near future, you may want to consider doing an options strategy with it. You can purchase the stock when the price is below market value (often for a much lower price because you just need to pay the premium upfront), and then sell it when it goes back up to market value or the market value goes up in general.

This is why options are a great investing strategy for those who are just getting started with swing trading. Some of the other strategies require a large amount of money upfront for you to see any profits and there are many beginners who are not able to do this. Options make it easier to get into the market and make a substantial profit even when your initial capital is so low.

Buying call options

So, let's take some time to look at the steps that you need to take in order to work with the options strategy. The first step is that you need to pick out the right stocks. This can be a big task for a beginner because there are so many of these available for you to trade on the New York Stock Exchange. The best way to deal with this is to create a good set of stocks that you will add to your watchlist, ones that you will use the most often when you are ready to trade. Having this list will limit you to just healthy stocks that work well with this strategy and can save you a ton of time over your trading experience.

From here, you will want to wait for outside moves or large percentage moves out of the stocks that you place in the watchlist. When these things start to happen with one or more of your stocks, it is time to use them to implement the options strategy. An even better thing to watch out for is if that big move is due to an earnings report and if there are some strong factors that move it. When this happens, it means that the stock price is changing because of strong fundamental reasons.

The next thing that you want to work on is assessing the market environment if you plan to do a buy call option in a bullish trend. As a trader, you need to have a good idea of the type of market you are in, otherwise, you will make poor decisions along the way. When you know the market, you will be able to decide if you would like to be on the long or the short side of the trade. The easiest way to tell if you are looking at a bullish trend is to look for a series of higher lows or higher highs. Outside of being able to determine how the market is doing overall, you need to also look at the characteristics of the market environment. This would include whether you are dealing with high volatility or low volatility. This can help you to pick the best expiration date for your options.

Now it is time to pick out the strike price that you want to work with. If you aren't sure what you are looking for, this can be a difficult task. Ideally, you want to pick an out of the money option, but it needs to be one that doesn't go too far out of the money. Out of the money is used to help describe the call option that has a strike price that is higher than the market price of that asset, or a put option that has a strike price that ends up being lower than the market price of the asset.

Next, you need to pick out your expiration time. The best options strategy is going to give your stock enough time to reach the strike price so that you can pay out for your call option, otherwise, it ends up expiring worthless. If the expiration time is too big, the risk decreases, but the potential profits are going to be smaller as well. Since you are working with swing trading, remember that your expiration dates will need to be within two weeks for this.

You also need to optimize your entries and exits and then buy on the pullbacks. As a rule of thumb, you should remember that this strategy is going to require a bit of time and you will need to have some patience before you see the results. If you are working with the call options, one tactic that can help you is to purchase on pullbacks. Either way, always define a maximum stop loss after you have purchased your option and then align the profit to where you believe the market is going to land before the option expires.

During the whole time of the trade, you will need to watch the market and manage things as needed. If the option ends up reaching your price ahead of time, you can always sell it out before the expiration date, but you need to do it at the right time.

During times when there is not a lot of volatility in the market, you will want to make sure to reduce your position when doing options. If at any time you think that your trade is still doing well but you just need a bit more time in order to see it succeed, you may want to consider rolling that option into another expiration date. This is something that a lot of traders can do, but you have to watch out for time decay. Time decay is just the ratio that will measure the changes in an options price relative to the decrease in time to expiration.

Using the swing trading option strategy can be a good investment strategy that will make you money. It does mean that you need to have some idea of how the market works in order to see success and for you to use it in the proper manner. There are times when the market is not going to move the way that you would like, and this can be disappointing. But for those who would like to limit their risks a little bit, and would like the opportunity to make bigger profits without having to bring as much money to the table, this can be one of the best ways to get started.

Chapter 6:

Strategy Three – Candlestick Charts

When it comes to investing in the stock market, one of the best strategies that traders like to work with is known as candlestick charts. The way that you read through these will vary based on the strategy that you want to work with and often the time frame that you use will vary as well. For example, with day trading you may only look at charts that are fifteen minutes or half an hour. But with swing trading, you may look at a chart for an hour or a few hours to make sure you are set.

The candlestick charts are a good technical tool to use because they will show a lot of data about your chosen stock all in one place. They can actually show more information than you are able to find a traditional stock chart and can be more useful than the options that just connect the closing prices together. When looking at these candlesticks are going to build up patterns that are able to predict where the price will go along the way and the colors that are added into the charts can make them easier for traders to read through.

When it comes to working with a candlestick patter there are a few types that you can work with. Choosing one will depend on the market that you want to work on. Whether you are dealing with a bearish market or a bullish market, there will be candlestick patterns that you can check out to help you pick out a good stock that will make you good money. It is also important to find some of your own candlestick patterns. If you only go and follow the ones that big hedge funds and other companies send out, you often will be sent in the wrong direction and you will not see the results that you want. Finding a candlestick pattern on your own in the market means that it is actually a good investment for you to follow.

Before we get much further, let's take a look at some of the best candlestick patterns that you can use, and which markets to use them in, to help you know how to get started. No matter how the market is doing or which stock you are working with, these patterns can help you to earn money with swing trading.

The first option that we will look at is known as the three-line strike. This is a bullish three-line strike reversal pattern. It is going to show you three black candles that are on a downtrend. Each of the bar posts at a lower low and then they will close near a new intrabar low. Then you will see a fourth bar that is going to start out lower than the other three, but it is going to end with a reversal out into a wide-range outside the bar that closes out above the high of the first candle that was in the series. You are going to notice that the opening print will also mark the low on the fourth bar.

When you see this reversal, it means that you are going to see a higher price coming up soon with that stock. If you look at some charts and see this pattern, you will be able to make a profit 80 percent of the time as long as you make a purchase before the price starts to go back up.

This one is the two black gapping candlesticks. This is an option that you can use in a bearish market and it is going to happen when the stock has gone through a big top in an uptrend and then there is going to be a gap down. This gap down is going to yield out two black bars that will post lower lows. With this pattern, you will be able to predict that the stock will keep going through a decline and depending on how big the trend is, it could show a downtrend in the market. If you notice this trend there is a big chance that the stock is going to get lower prices throughout the future.

If you see this option, you may want to consider whether it is time to enter the market or not. Some people like to enter the market at this time because they can get stocks at a good price. However, if you don't think that the market is going to go up within the next few weeks, this is not the best option to help you to do well with swing trading.

Another strategy that you may like is known as three black crows. This one will start out at or near the high of your uptrend. You will then notice that there are three black bars that are going to post at lower lows. This one is a candlestick that is going to predict that the stock will continue to decline for the foreseeable future. The version of this that is the most bearish is going to start at a new high point because it sometimes traps buyers and traders who want to enter on a momentum play. This pattern, though, is going to predict in most cases that the stock is going to stay with the lower prices for now and that it will not go back up at this point in time.

Some traders like to go with the evening star candlestick option for their strategy. This is another bearish strategy that is going to start with a white bar that is tall, and this is going to carry an uptrend which leads the stock to a new high. You will then notice that the market is going to gap up a bit higher on the next bar, but then there will be an issue without any new buyers joining the market. Because there aren't many buyers, you will notice a narrow range candlestick on the chart. Then there will be a gap down with the following bar to help complete the pattern. This is going to predict that the stock will see a decline, probably going way down.

If you see the evening star candlestick, it is going to show that there will be a downward trend with the stock and that it is not likely to go up right now until you see some reversals. If you think that some big news that will change up the market sometime soon, then this is a good time to enter the market because you will be able to get the stock for a really low price.

You can also work with the abandoned baby candlestick strategy. This is another bullish option that you can use, and it will appear at the low of a downtrend, right after there is a series of black candles that print out some new lows. The market is going to gap even lower on the next bar, but when there aren't any new sellers to help out, it is going to yield a narrow range Doji candlestick at the opening and closing prints at the same price. Then there will be a bullish gap on the third bar that will help to complete the pattern and it will predict that the recovery is going to continue to new highs. This is a good one to use when you are trying to see if the price is about to go up with the stock you want to work with.

No matter which option you are doing with candlesticks, you must make sure that you are able to read a lot of charts in the process. If you find research boring and you don't want to look for all these trends, you are going to run into some trouble with this investment option. It is all about the charts and knowing how to read them properly.

Of course, if you are able to go through these charts and you pick the right time frames, you may be surprised at how much information you are able to get out of these charts. Many of them are going to show some clear trends and can spell out the stocks that are about to do well. While others may just look at the closing information that comes with traditional charts for their stocks, they are missing out on a lot of the good information that is possible when working with candlestick charts.

Working with candlesticks can be a great way for you to figure out which way the market is going to go. They are not completely accurate all of the time, but they can give you a good idea of how the trend is going to continue in the near future and will give you a way to determine if it is time to get into the market or if you need to wait until a later time. Many people like to work with the candlestick strategies because this allows them to look at the market in an accurate way and make the best predictions on what is going to happen in the future.

Conclusion

Thanks for making it through to the end of this book, let's hope it was informative and able to provide you with all of the tools you need to achieve your goals whatever they may be.

The next step is to get to work with your own swing trading strategy. Swing trading can be the best option for you to use when it comes to making money in the market over the short-term. Unlike day trading that is going to take up all your time and can be really risky, swing trading will provide all the profit and all the benefits while giving you more freedom to do the trade and with less stress.

This guidebook provides you with the best tools that you need in order to get started with swing trading. Hopefully by now you have learned what swing trading is all about, how to get started with swing trading, and understand some of the benefits and tips that you can follow in order to do well with swing trading. We have provided you with three of the best strategies that you can use that will ensure that you will make money with swing trading.

When you are ready to make money in the stock market without having to wait years to take advantage of the money, then swing trading is the investment option for you. Make sure you have read through this guidebook to help you get started with swing trading today!

Finally, if you found this book useful in any way, a review on Amazon is always appreciated!

Description

Choosing the right investment option for yourself is never an easy task. There are so many options that you can choose from and everyone wants to be able to reduce their risks as much as possible. When it comes to increasing your profits and decreasing your risks over just a few weeks, swing trading is the right option for you.

This guidebook is going to provide you with all the information you need to get started with swing trading. Whether you have been investing for a long time or you are just getting started, you are sure to find the answers you need. Some of the topics that we will explore about swing trading in this guidebook include:

- What is swing trading?
- The benefits of swing trading
- How to get started with swing trading
- Breakouts and breakdowns
- The option strategy
- Candlestick charts

Making money in just a few weeks is possible as long as you know what you are doing. Check out this guidebook and learn just how swing trading can work for you!